Pray Like This ...

Sermons On The Lord's Prayer

Alex A. Gondola, Jr.

CSS Publishing Company, Inc., Lima, Ohio

PRAY LIKE THIS ...

Copyright © 2003 by
CSS Publishing Company, Inc.
Lima, Ohio

All rights reserved. No part of this publication may be reproduced in any manner whatsoever without the prior permission of the publisher, except in the case of brief quotations embodied in critical articles and reviews. Inquiries should be addressed to: Permissions, CSS Publishing Company, Inc., P.O. Box 4503, Lima, Ohio 45802-4503.

Scripture quotations marked (NRSV) are from the *New Revised Standard Version of the Bible*, copyright 1989 by the Division of Christian Education of the National Council of the Churches of Christ in the USA. Used by permission.

Scripture quotations marked (RSV) are from the *Revised Standard Version of the Bible*, copyrighted 1946, 1952 ©, 1971, 1973, by the Division of Christian Education of the National Council of the Churches of Christ in the USA. Used by permission.

Scripture quotations marked (TEV) are from the *Good News Bible*, in Today's English Version. Copyright © American Bible Society 1966, 1971, 1976. Used by permission.

Library of Congress Cataloging-in-Publication Data

Gondola, Alex A.,
   Pray like this— : sermons on the Lord's Prayer / Alex A. Gondola, Jr.
      p. cm.
   ISBN 0-7880-1942-2 (pbk. : alk. paper)
   1. Lord's prayer—Sermons. 2. United Church of Christ—Sermons. 3. Sermons, American. I. Title.
   BV230.G59 2003
   226.9'606—dc21

2003003527

For more information about CSS Publishing Company resources, visit our website at www.csspub.com or e-mail us at custserv@csspub.com or call (800) 241-4056.

ISBN 0-7880-1942-2   PRINTED IN U.S.A.

*Dedicated to
our son
Andrew David Gondola
in the hope
that he will always know
the Lord and his Prayer*

Acknowledgments

Someone has said Christianity is always just one generation from extinction. We usually receive the Good News because someone has passed it to us. For many of us, our spiritual formation began in childhood when a parent, grandparent, or other significant person taught — and encouraged — us to pray. I thank my parents, Alex and Elizabeth, grandparents and aunts and uncles for teaching me to pray.

Often a congregation strengthens and deepens a child's prayer life. I'm grateful for the Sunday school teachers, members, and pastors of The Congregational Church of Hollis, New Hampshire, my childhood church. One pastor, The Reverend Dr. Philip H. Mitchell, was especially significant in my spiritual development. For more than forty years, I've been proud to call Phil Mitchell both pastor and friend.

Individual parishioners, and especially the faithful prayer chains of churches I have served: Plymouth-Bethesda United Church of Christ in Utica, New York; Trinity United Church of Christ in Rome, New York; and The First Congregational Church (UCC) of West Springfield, Massachusetts, have taught me the power of prayer. The members and friends of Dennis Union Church (UCC) in Dennis, Massachusetts, continue to support my prayer life, my writing, and my family and me, as do colleagues The Reverend Dr. Constance Bickford, Hope Hardy, Virginia Haskell, Patricia Keeler, Steve Lovejoy, Noel Tipton, and Barbara Wells. I'm grateful for all the above.

I have listened to audiotapes, lectures, and sermons, read books and articles and attended workshops and retreats on prayer. All have been influential. I've tried to identify and credit every source. I'm grateful for every insight I have gained about prayer from whatever source.

My wife Bonnie, always my best reader, provided valuable corrections to this manuscript. Nancy McKiernan, Church Office Administrator, readied it for submission. Thanks also go to CSS

Publishing Company and particularly editors Thomas W. Lentz, Stan Purdum, and Teresa Rhoads. I'm proud to be associated with CSS Publishing Company, an important and growing resource for Christian education and formation.

In 2 Timothy, there is an account of the Apostle Paul writing to his young friend Timothy: "I am reminded of your sincere faith, a faith that lived first in your grandmother Lois and your mother Eunice and now, I am sure, lives in you" (1:5 NRSV). Like Timothy, we have received the faith, including instruction and encouragement in prayer. Perhaps part of our thanks to those who have encouraged our prayer life is simply finding ways to pass it on.

Table Of Contents

Preface	9
1. Introduction To The Lord's Prayer	11

The Petitions

2. "Our Father Who Art In Heaven"	15
3. "Hallowed Be Thy Name"	21
4. "Thy Kingdom Come"	27
5. "Thy Will Be Done"	33
6. "Give Us This Day Our Daily Bread"	39
7. "Forgive Us Our Debts As We Forgive Our Debtors"	45
8. "Lead Us Not Into Temptation"	51
9. "Deliver Us From Evil"	55
10. "For Thine Is The Kingdom And The Power And The Glory, Forever"	61
11. "Amen"	67

Preface

Countless books have been written on prayer — and on the Lord's Prayer. Why bother to write yet another? Perhaps an illustration might help answer that question. I heard this story from The Reverend Dr. John P. Webster some fifteen years ago. It's also found in one of his books, *Rekindle the Fire!* (Grenfell Reading Center, 1997, pp. 25-26).

John and his wife Phyllis had an old hand pump in the yard of their beautifully restored, nineteenth century white clapboard farmhouse in the Berkshires. With the farmhouse came an old deed, entitling its owners to water from a spring on a hill above. There was a length of pipe coming out of an old sink — but no water.

John searched for the spring. After considerable effort he came upon a length of rusty pipe which he followed to the spring. Apparently a wooden box had once enclosed the spring, but the wood in the box had rotted and caved in. Tree roots had grown over it and the spring was barely visible.

John went back down the hill and dragged up tools. He chopped and dug until the spring was uncovered. Later he hauled up fresh gravel to keep the spring fresh. Finally he hauled a tile pipe up the hill to line the bottom. Before long, pure cold water was again flowing down the hill, this time through a clean garden hose attached to the antique hand pump. The Websters could now enjoy refreshing water whenever they wanted.

Sometimes our prayer life can be like that old, covered-over spring: our "God connection" seems blocked. Perhaps approaching prayer from a different perspective — which may include reading about prayer — might help our spiritual life flow again. Jesus' disciples asked him, "Lord, teach us to pray" (Luke 11:1b RSV). They knew they needed to keep learning about prayer to keep growing in prayer. And so, I believe, do we.

I hope this book will prove a useful tool in opening or deepening prayer life. For the prayer that Jesus taught his disciples, the Lord's Prayer, promises living water direct from the Source.

1

Introduction To The Lord's Prayer

Text: Matthew 6:7-14

Many years ago the famous fable writer, Aesop, wrote, "Familiarity breeds contempt." Mark Twain had a comeback for that, you know: "Familiarity breeds contempt — and children!" But what Aesop wrote is true, isn't it? Don't we sometimes take the familiar for granted?

I think of a scene I once saw atop Mount Washington. My wife Bonnie and I were on vacation. It was our first trip ever to the summit. We were lucky. It was a clear August day. The view from the top was astonishing.

So I was amused to see one of the tour guides, seated on a rock, with his nose buried in a paperback book. That breathtaking view had become routine to him, maybe even boring. Sometimes what we take for granted is a familiar place.

Sometimes we take a familiar object for granted. A good illustration comes from one of my previous churches. There is, in Trinity United Church of Christ in Rome, New York, a small oil painting of the Holy Family: Mary, Joseph, and the Baby Jesus. It has hung on the wall just to the left of the pulpit since 1936 or 1937.

The little painting has no title, no artist's name, no indication of who gave it. It just hung there on the wall, largely overlooked, for fifty years until a new member, who was interested in art, began to ask questions. She encouraged us to get a local art expert to look at it. Later slides and a description were mailed to Sotheby's of London.

It turns out the painting was done in the late 1600s or early 1700s in Genoa or Venice. It's the work of a master. And rather valuable, too: $20,000 in 1980s dollars, much more today. It took the sharp eye of a new member to notice the hidden value in a familiar thing.

The Lord's Prayer is also familiar, isn't it? After all, most of us have known it since childhood. We've recited it thousands of times. We could say it in our sleep. Yet like the view from atop Mount Washington, like the little painting in my previous church, the Lord's Prayer is a treasure. Tertullian, one of the Early Church Fathers, called it "The gospel abbreviated." Distinguished Professor John Killinger calls it "the most effective summary of Christian theology ever given." High praise for a prayer you can recite in thirty seconds!

A billion Christians recite the Lord's Prayer. There's *never* an instant when it isn't being offered up somewhere in some language. But how many of us have actually *studied* it? We'll take one petition of the Lord's Prayer per month, until we've studied it all. We'll consider questions like "Does 'Lead us not into temptation' mean God *tempts* us?" We'll look at why the Roman Catholics have a different version than Protestants. By the end of this series, we'll be even more familiar with the "Our Father." But that familiarity, I hope, will breed, not contempt, but a new appreciation and a new power in our praying the Lord's Prayer.

For prayer *does have* power, although we sometimes discount it. I once heard the story of a small town where a nightclub opened on Main Street. This nightclub caused a lot of controversy in that town, rather like the introduction of "exotic dancers" at Guido Murphy's bar on Main Street in Hyannis. The only church in town held an all-night prayer vigil. The church members prayed that God would put an end to the club. That very night, the nightclub was struck by lightning. It burned completely down. The owners of the club sued the church for destruction of property. The church leaders denied being responsible. When the case came to court, the judge made this observation: The nightclub owners apparently believed in the power of prayer. But the church leaders apparently did not!

Oswald Chambers writes, "Every time we pray, our horizon is altered, our attitude to things is altered, not sometimes but every time, and the amazing thing is that we don't pray more." Martin

Luther, mighty in prayer, proclaimed, "I have often learned more in one prayer than I have been able to glean from much reading and reflection." Abraham Lincoln believed in the power of prayer. He said, during the turmoil of the Civil War, "I have been driven many times to my knees by the overwhelming conviction that I had nowhere else to go." Prayer is mighty. But I know too often I don't take the time or make the effort to "hook up" with God in prayer. Maybe you don't, either.

Herbert Jackson, a foreign missionary, describes how, when he was newly "out in the field," he was assigned an automobile that wouldn't start without a push. So for two years he got someone to push-start his car in the morning so he could get going. Then all day, as Jackson made his rounds in his mission station, he either kept the motor running or parked the car on a hill. That way he could be certain to get it going again.

After two years his replacement came to relieve him. Herbert Jackson proudly explained his ingenious tricks for making his car run. The new missionary wasn't impressed. Instead he looked under the hood. After a moment's searching he found a loose cable, twisted it slightly, and the car started immediately!

The power was there all the time! But the connection was loose. God's power: the power to guide us, the power to comfort us, the power to heal us, the power to make us whole when we're *not* healed, is always available. But we may discount it. We may not connect with it. We may not utilize prayer's power.

But Jesus did. Over and over again in the Gospels Jesus is depicted at prayer. He began his public ministry with forty days of prayer and fasting in the desert. He often went off to a quiet place to pray. Sometimes Jesus prayed all night. He found prayer more rejuvenating than sleep.

He prayed before he fed 5,000 with five loaves and two fish. He prayed before he healed the sick. He prayed for his followers. He prayed for courage to face suffering. Jesus prayed with such power that his face began to shine.

Have *you* ever run into a person whose prayer life is so deep, whose God-connectedness is so solid, that his or her face shines with light? *I* have. In fact, we have *several* of these shining "saints" in our church.

His disciples saw what Jesus could do. More importantly, they saw who he *was*. He prayed. The blind began to see. He prayed. The lame danced. He prayed. And 5,000 were fed. He prayed. The wind and the waves were stilled. He prayed. Guilt drained from the faces of men and women he had forgiven. Finally the disciples got it! Jesus' power was connected to prayer!

So one day, after Jesus had been praying, and his face was still shining, one of them rushed up and begged him fervently, "Lord, teach *us* the secret of contentment. Lord, teach us to be brave, like you. Lord, teach us what is *really* important!"

"Lord, teach us to pray!"

And he did.

Let's not take the Lord's Prayer for granted. Let's not discount its power. For "more things are wrought by prayer than this world dreams of," as Tennyson said. I know I need to grow in my prayer life. I know my face is not always shining. I know I could do more if I prayed more. Maybe you know the same things. So I'm looking forward to studying the one prayer that Jesus taught us: the Lord's Prayer. I hope you are, too.

2

"Our Father Who Art In Heaven"

One day in India, a boy came upon a Holy Man praying by the banks of the Ganges River. When the Holy Man was finished praying, the boy went over to him and asked him, "Sir, will you teach *me* to pray?" The Holy Man immediately grabbed the boy by his head and shoulders and dunked his head completely under water in the Ganges. The boy's arms flailed frantically, as he struggled to break free and to breathe again. Finally the Holy Man released his hold. The boy came to the surface. When he was able to speak again he shouted, "Why did you *do that* to me?"

The Holy Man answered, "I just gave you your first lesson. When you long to pray as much as you longed to breathe when your head was under water, then, and only then, can I begin to teach you to pray" (this story has circulated in a variety of forms for years). Aren't you glad that Holy Man wasn't your teacher in Sunday school?

What a contrast between the Holy Man's approach and that of Jesus! Twenty centuries ago one of Jesus' disciples came upon Jesus in prayer. He saw the serenity shining in Jesus' face. He longed to know what it was like to be that God-connected. So when Jesus was done praying, the disciple approached him and begged Jesus, "Lord, teach us to pray."

What was *Jesus'* response? No dramatics, no dunking, no near drowning. No, I imagine Jesus smiled. Perhaps he had been just waiting for someone to ask. I imagine he gathered all twelve of his disciples around him. I imagine, still smiling, he said, "Pray like this." And the first words Jesus taught his disciples to pray were, "Our Father who art in heaven." No struggle or long salutation, just six simple words. But if you and I can really pray those six simple words, then we already know the secret of prayer.

For Jesus taught his disciples — and us — to call God "Father." Sounds so familiar to us today, doesn't it? But in Jesus' day it was astonishing. For in all of Hebrew Scripture, 750 pages, in all of the "Old Testament," God is called "Father" only seven times! But *every time* Jesus speaks of God — except once, when Jesus was apparently quoting a Psalm (Psalm 22:1/Matthew 27:46) — but *every time* Jesus speaks of God — 170 times in all — Jesus calls God "Father." And the phrase he always uses for "Father" is "Abba." Say it with me softly, please, "Abba, Abba." What does it sound like? To me it sounds like one of a baby's first words, "DaDa." Or maybe little children calling their father "Daddy."

There's a touching story told about John F. Kennedy, Jr. After JFK's assassination, the little boy, of course, missed his dad. One thing he especially missed was the way JFK used to throw him up in the air and catch him. So one day "John-John" went up to an aide named William Haddad and asked, "Are you a daddy?" Haddad admitted he was a dad. "Then will you throw me up in the air?" asked "John-John." You see, to John F. Kennedy, Jr., a "dad" was someone who threw you in the air, and someone you could trust to catch you on the way down. Jesus wants us to call God "Daddy" like that: trusting God and knowing God is completely approachable. For his astonishing revelation is that God is our Dad.

But what if we had a dad who was less than perfect? I'm a dad myself. I'm not perfect. Ask our son Andrew. He'll tell you I'm not perfect — unless it's one of those days when I'm perfectly wrong about everything! Some of us may even have had a dad who was absent, neglectful, or abusive. How can we call God "Father" if our memories of Dad are bad? We need to remember Jesus wasn't using his own "father," Joseph the carpenter of Nazareth, or of any other *human* father, as a model. He taught us to pray, "Our Father *which art in heaven*." The word "heaven" comes from the old Anglo-Saxon word "heave on," which means "lift up." All earthly fathers are imperfect. But our "lifted up," spiritual Father is perfect. Jesus wants us to talk to God as if God were our perfect parent — a perfect father and perfect mother rolled up into One.

But Jesus did teach us to call God "Daddy." We can approach God with the trust a little child would approach a perfect mother or dad. What does that mean, then, if God is our "Dad"?

First, if God is our (perfect) *Father*, then you and I will never ever be forgotten. Recently the *Cape Cod Times* indicated that there are now over six billion people on earth. Imagine: six thousand million souls! With six billion people on the planet, we may wonder how God could possibly know us. We can be like the little boy who couldn't quite get the Lord's Prayer right. He prayed, "Our Father which art in heaven, *how'd you know my name?*"

But God is a devoted Dad who both knows us *and* loves us. Jesus assures us that God knows us so completely even the hairs on our heads are numbered (Luke 12:7). The average number of hairs on the human head, by the way, according to a Max Factor survey, is 110,000. Some of us may have dramatically more hair. Some of us may have dramatically less hair. But whether we have two hairs on our head, or 200,000, be certain God knows the number. God knows us and loves us individually, down to the roots of our hair.

Plus if God is our heavenly Father, God cares about us enough to guide us. James Hewett, a retired Presbyterian pastor, writes about how he was guided by a loving dad. When Hewett was a small boy, growing up in rural Pennsylvania, his parents would take him to visit his grandparents. They lived at a distance of several miles. Often they walked.

One night a thick fog settled over the hilly country. As a small boy, Hewett was terrified of walking home in the darkness and fog. But his mother reassured him, "Don't worry. Your father knows the way." You see, Hewett's father had traveled that same country road for many years: during the war years, when he walked because gasoline was rationed; during his youth when he biked to court Hewett's mother. Hewett's Father had already been there. He knew every twist and turn of the road.

Hewett writes, "How often when I can't see the road of life, and have felt that familiar panic rising in my heart have I heard the echo of my mother's voice: 'Don't worry. Your Father knows the way' " (*Illustrations Unlimited*, Tyndale House Publishers,

Inc., p. 201). If God is our Father, God cares enough to guide us. When the way ahead of us is dark or uncertain, we can put our hand in the hand of a loving Father who knows the way.

Finally, God not only knows us, and guides us, but also can provide for us. God is a loving Parent strong enough to meet all our legitimate needs. President Teddy Roosevelt was a strong man and a strong father, too, to his six children. But there was one child, Alice, who apparently was really wild. Alice's antics scandalized the staid Washington, D.C., of Roosevelt's time.

One day Alice kept racing in and out of the Oval Office while her father was conducting important business with a prominent visitor. The President's guest complained about Alice's frequent interruptions. He asked Teddy Roosevelt to make her stop. T. R. responded, "I can be President of the United States or I can control Alice. (But) I can't possibly do both." Even the strongest human father can't provide for all our needs: disciplinary, physical, emotional, and spiritual. But God is the kind of Dad who has both the power and the love to help us in every way.

The secret of prayer is to pray believing in our heart of hearts that God *is* our Father, a perfect loving parent that you and I can approach with confidence at any time. A loving Dad who knows us, will guide us, and can provide for us.

John Killinger writes:

> *What a difference (that awareness) makes in the life of prayer! ... When one realizes that (God) is our Father, one can do nothing else but pray. Not have time to pray? Why when we have discovered our true relationship to (God), we shall want to pray all the time. Not know how to pray? Why, no one has trouble talking or listening to a real Father. When we are able to say, "Our Father" and know it and mean it with all sincerity, prayer becomes ... the most natural activity in the world ... Then we would rather pray than eat or sleep or watch television, for prayer is our line of connection to the heavenly Father. (The God Named Hallowed*, Abingdon Press, p. 21)

Okay, so maybe most of us aren't like that! Maybe our prayer life is pretty spotty. Maybe it's almost non-existent. Still, as G. K. Chesterton put it, "Anything worth doing is worth doing badly." We can start praying in a new way today.

"Lord, teach us to pray." "Pray like this, 'Our Father which art in heaven.' " Six simple words that can change our entire perspective on living. God is our Dad, our perfect Parent, who knows us, can provide for us, and who longs to guide us. Place your hand in God's hand like a little child. Trust God. For your Father knows the way.

3

"Hallowed Be Thy Name"

My previous church in West Springfield — like this one — was located next to a graveyard. Only in West Springfield the graves came right up to the side of the church itself. It was a grave sight! If you were bored with the sermon, and glanced out the window, you likely faced an eighteenth century carving of the Grim Reaper!

Church volunteers maintained that cemetery for years. They lovingly cared for the ancient stones, some of which were 250 years old. They cut the grass. They pulled the weeds. They pruned the bushes and repaired the wrought-iron fences.

That ancient burial ground was treated with respect. It was, in fact, an oasis of green in a somewhat run-down part of town. Still, every Halloween, it was also a potential target. The Trustees knew this. They kept the gates locked. The cemetery was well lit. The police did their best to patrol it. Actually, police coverage around the church was always excellent. One sergeant in my congregation attributed it to our strategic location: one block from the Station House and two doors from Dunkin' Donuts!

Unfortunately, one Halloween, vandals did get into the cemetery. They turned over or broke some of the ancient stones. They spray-painted some of the modern monuments, too.

I remember going out to the cemetery the morning after Halloween. Ed was with me. Ed was a seventy-year member. Most of Ed's family was buried in that graveyard. Ed and his wife would be buried in that cemetery, too. The old gentleman was clearly pained when he saw the damaged stones. I remember his eyes misting with anger and frustration as he asked, "Alex, isn't *anything* sacred anymore?"

"Isn't anything sacred anymore?" That's a good question! I'm not a social conservative. But I sometimes wonder myself. For it seems to me many things we used to hold in reverence just aren't respected. Take, for example, the Oval Office at the White House. Some presidents wouldn't even take off their suit coats or loosen their ties while in that room. Yet we all know how the Oval Office and its surrounding rooms have been misused. One result, I think, could be an erosion of respect for the Presidency of the United States.

Take the men who used to be the role models of my childhood: Christopher Columbus, George Washington, and Thomas Jefferson among them. Every schoolchild was taught to honor them. Goodbye, Columbus! In twenty years his reputation has changed from courageous explorer to exploiter of indigenous peoples. Washington and Jefferson don't shine with quite the same luster anymore either. For most of us now know more about these "Fathers of our Country" and their sex lives than we really care to know.

Take the American flag. When I was in elementary school, flag raising and flag lowering was a big daily ceremony. It took four people either to raise or to lower the flag: one child to hold it, one child to fold it, one child to salute it, and a teacher to oversee. It was an honor to be chosen to raise or lower the flag. Often the teacher granted it as a reward for good behavior. I myself got to raise the flag about twice.

Heaven help you if you accidentally let the flag touch the ground or didn't fold it correctly! We thought lightning would strike us dead! But (until the recent patriotic revival after the events of September 11, 2001) I would guess flag raising and lowering was not a ceremony at most of our schools until recently. It just was not considered important.

I could go on: a loss of reverence for life (children killing children), the erosion of marriage, the breakup of the family, our abuse of the planet (which Native Americans considered sacred). But you know the problems all too well. Ed's question raised the day after Halloween in that desecrated graveyard is still valid: Isn't there *anything* sacred anymore?

But then we come to our Lord's Prayer and its very first petition. Jesus said to his disciples and us, "Pray like this; Our Father who art in heaven, *hallowed be thy name*" (Matthew 6:9 RSV). To "hallow" means "to respect greatly," "to make holy or set apart," "to venerate," or "to hold sacred."

The first thing we should ask for in prayer is that God be respected. Our duty is to honor God, even before we pray for our daily bread. Is anything sacred? The name of God is!

Now there's more to this petition than just not cursing. Although the Third Commandment says God is not pleased when we take God's name in vain, we ask God to damn a hammer. How foolish! We want the Creator of the Universe to curse an inanimate object? That's disrespectful and an abuse of God's name. And if it hurts us when our good names are misused, can't we also assume using God's name as a curse is hurtful to God?

President Woodrow Wilson's father was a distinguished Presbyterian minister. Dr. Wilson once was with a group of men who were having a heated debate. In the midst of the argument one of the men took the Lord's name in vain. Then he realized Dr. Wilson, the Presbyterian pastor, the President's father, was there. The man apologized profusely to the pastor. To which Dr. Wilson responded, "It is not to me that you owe your apology, but to God" (reported in *The Lord's Prayer* by Clarence Macartney, Fleming H. Revell Company, p. 26).

Hallowing the name of God means not cursing. But it's more than just not cursing. It is treating God with the measure of respect God truly deserves. God deserves to be respected because God is our Creator. The Psalmist says the moon and the stars are the work of God's hands. Psalm 8: "O Lord, our Lord, how majestic is thy name in all the earth" (v. 1 RSV). God raised up the mountains and poured out the oceans. The skies above us, with their white clouds and deep blues and pinks and grays at sunset, are the canvas of God. "The sky is ... daily bread of (our) eyes," writes Emerson.

Every blade of grass is infused with the goodness of God. Spring is God's way of saying, "Do it again! Do it again!" "Earth's crammed with heaven, and every common bush afire with God," writes Elizabeth Barrett Browning.

Another poet, Joyce Kilmer, writes in a poem we all learned as children:

> *I think that I shall never see*
> *A poem as lovely as a tree.*

*A tree whose hungry mouth is pressed
Against the earth's sweet flowing breast.*

*Poems are made by fools like me.
But only God can make a tree.*

The other day, I sat on the steps of the bandstand on the Town Common. It was dark. The October wind was rustling in the trees. I noticed the trees. It occurred to me that human beings can land a man on the moon, launch a space shuttle, create complicated computer networks. But nothing we have made yet compares to the wonder of a single tree.

God deserves to be respected because God is our Creator: a wonderful, astonishing Creator. "O Lord, our Lord, how majestic is thy name in all the earth!" You have surrounded us with beauty. Hallowed be thy name.

And God is not only our Creator but also our Sustainer. You and I couldn't exist for even an instant, except that God holds us in life. Take a breath. Take a nice deep breath. Take another one. Feels good, doesn't it? Every breath we draw is a gift from God. "O Lord, our Lord, how majestic is thy name in all the earth!" You are the God who keeps us alive! Hallowed be thy name.

And God not only made us and sustains us, but God also claims us. The Bible, all 1,000-plus pages of it, is a record of God's love. A love that enfolds us like a mother enfolds her baby in her arms after birth. "Can a woman forget her own baby and not love the child that she bore? Even if a mother should forget her child, I will never forget you," promises God (Isaiah 49:15 TEV).

God's love is a love for us that will not let us go. It's a love that will even suffer and die for us on a Cross. God made us and sustains us and claims us and loves us. "O Lord, our Lord, how majestic is thy name in all the earth." God is far kinder to us than we deserve. Hallowed be thy name.

Hallowing God is respecting God as Creator and Sustainer. It's accepting the love that God has for each of us. But hallowing God is also, in a strange way, keeping our distance. It's recognizing the appropriate separation between our Creator and us. That's one thing I get from the story of Moses and God assigned for today.

In this wonderful, ancient passage, 3,000 or so years old, Moses meets God in the Tent of Meeting. They talk face to face, like two old friends. God's relationship with Moses is open and easy. Moses dares to question God. And God doesn't get angry. Moses even talks God into changing God's mind. Moses is very close to God. But even in this intimate relationship there remains a distance. Moses is creature and God remains God. Moses begs to see God's face. He loves God. He's close to God. He longs to know God completely.

But God can't show Moses the fullness of God's glory. You and I can't see God and live, at least not in this life. God's holiness and power would be overwhelming to weak, sinful creatures like us. The most Moses is allowed to see is a glimpse of God's back. Even then Moses must be hidden in the cleft of a rock.

There's truth in that old story. God *is* our Creator and Sustainer and Lover: closer than breathing, nearer than our hands and feet. But God is also Other. God's distance and God's mystery are also a sign of God's love. We need to respect that distance and treat God and God's name with honor.

Is nothing sacred anymore? At least *one thing* should be. John Killinger writes that reverence for God is like a tent pole that holds up everything else. When we don't honor God, the tent pole collapses, and everything else starts falling down around us.

But when we respect God as Creator, Sustainer, Lover, and Other, when we put God first in all things, when we seek to hallow God by doing God's will for us, our lives find a supportive center and everything else begins to fall into its proper place (*The God Named Hallowed*, Abingdon Press, pp. 27, 29).

Praying "Our Father, who art in heaven, hallowed be your name" every day — praying "(God) Your reputation is at stake in me today. May I live in such a way as to do Your person great credit" (W. Phillip Keller, *A Layman Looks at the Lord's Prayer*, Worldwide Publications, p. 56) is important.

Hallowing the name of God with our words and deeds is raising the tent pole. It is the first step in recovering a sense of the sacredness of all of life.

4

"Thy Kingdom Come"

Many of us are familiar with Stephen Covey's 1989 bestseller, *The Seven Habits of Highly Effective People*. Covey begins his book with a personal illustration. He writes:

> *I remember a mini-paradigm shift I experienced one Sunday morning on a subway in New York. People were sitting quietly — some reading newspapers, some lost in thought, some resting with their eyes closed. It was a calm, peaceful scene.*
>
> *A man and his children entered the car. The children were soon yelling back and forth, throwing things, even grabbing people's papers. It was very disturbing. And yet, the father sitting next to me did nothing.*
>
> *It was difficult not to feel irritated. I could not believe he could be so insensitive as to let his children run wild ... It was easy to see that everyone else on the subway felt irritated, too. So finally, with what I felt was unusual patience ... I asked, "Sir, your children are really disturbing a lot of people. I wonder if you couldn't control them a little more?"*
>
> *The man lifted his gaze as if coming to ... consciousness ... and said softly, "Oh, you're right. I guess I should do something about it. We just came from the hospital where their mother died about an hour ago ... I guess they don't know how to handle it either."*
>
> *Can you imagine what I felt at that moment? Suddenly I saw things differently, I thought differently, I felt differently, I behaved differently. My irritation vanished ... My heart was filled with the man's pain. Feelings of sympathy and compassion flowed freely. "Your wife just died? Oh, I'm so sorry! Can you tell me about it? What can I do to help?"*[1]

Stephen Covey saw things differently, felt differently, and behaved differently *because of a changed perspective*. The children weren't acting out because they were wild. They were acting out their grief. The father wasn't overly lenient. He was overwhelmed by loss. A psychologist might say Stephen Covey "re-framed" the situation. Covey calls it a "paradigm shift."

We'll get back to Stephen Covey and paradigm shifts in a moment. But first let's think a bit about the Kingdom of God. We hear of it in our hymns: "I Love Thy Kingdom, Lord." We pray for it in our prayers: "Thy Kingdom come, thy will be done on earth as it is in heaven." We *know* the Kingdom of God was central to Jesus' preaching.

But honestly — on a day-to-day level — what *does* the Kingdom of God *have to do with us*? Americans haven't had a king since 1776. The Australians just voted to keep their Queen. But I don't think Americans would vote to rejoin the British Empire, do you? That would somehow seem like moving backwards. Kings and kingdoms are foreign to most of us. The king *I* encounter most is Burger King! Or maybe Larry King on television.

"The Kingdom of God"? It may sound a bit archaic, or maybe make believe, or maybe otherworldly, or maybe far distant. Perhaps *we* need one of Stephen Covey's paradigm shifts: a new perspective, a different way of thinking about the Kingdom of God.

What did Jesus mean when he taught us to pray for the Kingdom? One thing he meant was to open ourselves up to radical, personal change. For if *God* is our King (or Ruler, if you will), then you and I can no longer be the center of our own little universe. We'll have to climb down off our self-made throne.

Of course, most of us aren't as blatantly self-centered as Muhammad Ali was during his "I am the greatest" period. A colleague, irritated by Ali's perpetual boasting, once asked the boxer how good he was at golf. "I am the greatest at golf," announced Ali. "I just haven't tried it yet."

Another time he got on a plane and refused to buckle his seatbelt. "Superman don't need no seatbelt," Ali told the flight attendant. She responded, "Superman don't need no airplane, either." Ali buckled his belt.

Maybe we're not as self-absorbed as that. Maybe our self-centeredness is a little more subtle, like the novelist who said to a friend, "We've talked about *me* long enough. Now let's talk about you. Tell me, what do you think of my latest book?"

Still, many of us — if we were honest — would have to admit that it is tempting, much of the time, to put ourselves first. It's often our needs, our desires, our perspective, and our opinions that count most.

Much of our life is like a series of concentric circles. Too often we put ourselves at the center. The needs of our family and friends come next. Next come the needs of our community and the concerns of our country. And the Kingdom of God — if it's anywhere — is somewhere out on the edge.

But to pray, "Thy Kingdom come, thy will be done, on earth as it is in heaven" — and really mean it — is to reverse our focus. It's to put God's will first, the needs of others second, and our needs last.

A famous rabbi once surprised some scholars who were staying with him by asking them the question. "Where does God live?" The learned scholars laughed. "Obviously," they said, "God doesn't live in any one specific place. God is everywhere. The whole world is full of God's glory."

But the rabbi offered them a different perspective. He said, "God lives in the hearts of men and women who let God in." God lives in the hearts of men and women who let God in.

God is only King (Ruler) of our lives if we let God in. You and I are the *only* ones who can give God that central place. To pray "Thy Kingdom come" is not to pray for some indefinite spiritual state that will come in the far-distant future. Nor is it to pray for a political system that disappeared in the nineteenth century.

No, it means to pray for a change of perspective *now*. It's saying, "God, I invite you into my life. I put *you* in the center. I'll try my best to be your obedient subject. Please, you be the King."

That means King over everything, including our money. Luther said the last thing baptized in many of us is our wallet! Yet the love of money or an obsessive concern about money can come between us and God's rule. Sometimes an excessive anxiety over even a little bit of money can blind us totally to the beauty and goodness of God's world.

Try an experiment. After church, take a drive over to the overlook at Corporation Beach by the snack bar. It's beautiful there, isn't it? You get a 200-degree panoramic view of Cape Cod Bay. Take a moment to admire the mile-long stretch of white beach. Drink in the clouds above you and the waves below you. Then take two dimes and put them in front of your eyes! Two thin dimes can block out the sand, the sea, and the sky. I'm told a hundred-dollar bill works even better!

To pray, "Thy Kingdom come, thy will be done, on earth as it is in heaven," is to put God first in all things, including how we manage our money. *That* can seem kind of scary. Yet what God wants for each of us — symbolized by the Kingdom of God — is really what's best for us. For we are most truly ourselves the more we give of ourselves to God. As Augustine put it, "Our hearts will be restless until they find their rest in Thee." Abundant life comes from putting God first in all things, including money.

To me, Frances Havergal, author of the hymn, "Take My Life And Let It Be," is an excellent example. She was born into a wealthy, cultured, and distinguished British family. Her father was a prominent Anglican clergyman. Frances herself was brilliant.

By age four she was reading — and memorizing — the Bible. She eventually learned the entire New Testament — and much of the Old — by heart. Frances was an avid student, writer, and composer. She was a concert pianist much in demand. She mastered six languages. She was one of Stephen Covey's "Highly Effective People."

Frances Havergal had a distinguished background, a brilliant mind, and an engaging personality. Frances could have done almost anything. But in early adolescence she gave her life to God. She wrote, "I committed my soul to the Savior — and earth and heaven seemed brighter from that moment." You see, she had a paradigm shift. She devoted her considerable talents to doing God's work.

She wrote hymns. She taught Sunday school to servants. She tended to the poor personally. She even gave away her wealth.

There's a line in "Take My Life and Let It Be" that's missing in our hymnal. It goes: "Take my silver and my gold, not a mite will I withhold."

Frances Havergal lived that line. She sold all her jewelry — described as "fit for a countess" — to support Christian missions. She wrote, "I don't think I ever packed a box with such pleasure," as she sent off her jewels.

Unfortunately, her health was poor. She died at 42. Her favorite Bible verse was at the foot of her bed where she could see it when she died.

How would *you* measure the life of Frances Havergal? Some might say, "She never married. She died young; what a waste. She should have looked out more for herself, maybe held onto and enjoyed her possessions."

Others might say, "What a highly effective life. She put God first and did a lot of good. Her hymn moves us even 150 years after she wrote it."

I guess it depends on your perspective. At every instant we're offered a choice: the Kingdom of God or the kingdom of this world. But sometimes we need a paradigm shift to see what is *really* important.

"When you pray," said Jesus, "pray like this: thy Kingdom come." Invite God into your life. Say, with Frances Havergal, "Take my life and let it be, Consecrated, Lord, to Thee. Take my moments and my days. Let them flow in ceaseless praise."

She gave her life to God. And God gave it back to her in greater joy and abundance. You might be surprised what God can do in and through you and me, if we live in the Kingdom of God.

---

1. Reprinted with the permission of Simon & Schuster from *The Seven Habits of Highly Effective People* by Stephen R. Covey. Copyright © 1989 by Stephen R. Covey.

5

"Thy Will Be Done"

All of us are familiar with word association. Someone shouts out a word or a phrase, and we try to register our first reaction. For example, what do you think of (you don't have to *say* anything, but what do you *think of*) when I say, "Mother-in-law"? Some of you smile, maybe especially the mothers-in-law among us. Others maybe cringe.

We've all heard mother-in-law jokes and stories. We know the mother-in-law stereotype: bossy, meddling, threatening, right? But when *I* think of mothers-in-law, *I* think of *mine*, Elizabeth Coles Harris, an intelligent, attractive, kindly woman whom (because we lived in the same small town) I have known for forty years. By the way, I'm sending my mother-in-law a copy of this sermon.

Let's try another. How do you respond to "Thy will be done"? Again you don't have to answer out loud. But *what* do you think of when you hear that phrase? Perhaps the Lord's Prayer? Maybe Jesus' struggle in the Garden of Gethsemane? Or that phrase carved into a tombstone, as it sometimes was in earlier times? Maybe you connect "Thy will be done" with a shrug of resignation ("Well, if God really *wants* it, I guess I'll just have to put up with it"). Like "mother-in-law," "Thy will be done" may bring forth a variety of associations, some of which might not be positive.

The will of God: it's a big subject. This morning I'd like to offer four propositions about the will of God. I'm testing out these propositions. I'd be interested in your response to them, and/or *your* ideas about the will of God.

Proposition one: "Thy will be done" is one prayer that will *always* be answered! For God's will will always get done. After all, God's will is already perfectly followed in nature. God willed, God created a solar system where the earth revolves around the sun. So on earth we see the sun rise every morning and set every evening: God's will. God willed the tides to flow and the plants to grow and the snow to fall. So they do.

God's will *is* done in nature. And the Bible says God's will is done in heaven. Scripture portrays heaven as that blessed and happy place where God is always obeyed. One old Scottish preacher warns we'd better get used to obeying God *now*. Otherwise we won't feel at all comfortable in heaven!

Eventually God's will *will* be done on earth as it *is* in heaven. God has a plan for creation and humankind. It's called the Kingdom or Rule or Realm of God. Sooner or later, Thy will will be done. The question is, will *we* be the ones to do God's will — or will someone else?

Proposition two: God's will is always *good* for us. "Thy will be done" may sometimes sound grim. But note this: There are two Greek words for "will" in the Bible. One Greek word for God's will means "good pleasure." God's will is God's "good pleasure." God's will is, as one person put it, "catastrophically good."

God is on the side of wholesomeness and health, safe streets, a clean environment, honest business practices, good marriages, happy families, and polite children. God wants the same things we want. God wants what is best.

Dr. Samuel Shoemaker writes,

> *If the Kingdom of God were a box of cereal, the list of ingredients on the back would read: forgiveness of sins, welcome of the outcast, feeding the hungry, sharing what we have, loving our enemies, a community of friends, peace, righteousness, and joy in the Holy Spirit.*
> ("The Will of God," *Library of Distinctive Sermons*, vol. 8, Multnomah Publishers, p. 281)

We have nothing to fear from the will of God. It's good.

But maybe some of us are wondering, "If God's will is so good, why are there natural disasters in Honduras? Why are millions of children starving?" The problem of evil: that's really another whole sermon, or a whole series of sermons. But let me say briefly, God does not will evil. It's *not*, for example, God's will that little children should starve. In fact, God, like a loving parent, has already provided plenty of food to feed *all* God's children.

It's just that six percent of the world's population (we Americans) presently hold fifty percent of the world's wealth. If half the people in the world suffer from malnutrition (and they do) and eighty percent live in sub-standard housing (and they are), and we Americans are holding onto fifty percent of the world's wealth (and we do), whose fault is it that children are starving? It seems to me the blame falls on us, and not on God. God's will is always good and always right. The question is: "Are *we* right with God?"

Proposition three: God's will continues to be good, even when we don't understand it. Lots of things happen in our lives we don't understand. Some ask themselves, "Why did my loved one die? Why did I get cancer? Why does my son or daughter or sister or brother seem stuck in an unhappy marriage?"

One explanation that comforts *me* when *I* don't understand something is that my view is limited. But *God* sees the big picture always. *We* have a tendency to focus on the immediate. But *God* considers the ultimate. It's like an illustration Charles Allen uses about two boys in school (see *God's Psychiatry*, Spire Books, p. 105).

It is the will of their teacher that both boys do their homework. One boy does his homework, three hours every day after school. The other boy goofs off, plays video games, and watches television. Eventually the second boy fails and drops out of school.

Twenty years later, which boy is better off? The rebellious boy enjoyed his freedom in the short run. But he has trouble finding and keeping a job. The studious boy is freer, happier, and finds life more fulfilling because he learned his lessons and is better prepared. It's like the old saying: "The lazy student always does the most work."

God is like the teacher in that illustration. God knows what is ultimately for the best. Or take another illustration from baseball. In his book, *How Life Imitates the World Series*, Dave Bosewell writes about how Baltimore Orioles' manager Earl Weaver handled Reggie Jackson.

Weaver had a rule that no one could steal a base unless he was given the steal sign. This upset superstar Reggie Jackson. He felt he was fast enough and savvy enough to make his own decisions. One game he decided to steal a base *without getting* the steal sign. And Reggie did indeed steal second base.

Later Weaver took Jackson aside and explained why he didn't give the steal sign at that time. The next batter was Lee May, his best power hitter, after Jackson himself. When Jackson stole second, that left first open. So the pitcher intentionally walked May, taking the bat out of his hand.

The following batter wasn't strong against that particular pitcher. So Weaver felt he had to send in a pinch hitter to try to drive in the men on base. That left Weaver without bench strength later in the game when he needed it. Reggie Jackson only saw his *immediate* situation — the opportunity to steal second base. But Earl Weaver, the manager, saw the whole game (story recounted in *Illustrations for Preaching and Teaching from Leadership Journal*, Craig Brian Larson, editor, Baker Books, p. 167). Sometimes *we* think *we* know what is best. But God, seeing the big picture, knows what is even better. The will of God is always good, even though we may not immediately understand it.

Proposition four: If God's will will always be done, and God's will is always good, even when we don't understand it, then the best thing we can do for ourselves and for others is to do it. As Dante put it, "In (God's) will is our peace."

How do we *know* the will of God for us? That's another question worthy of another whole sermon. However I can say, briefly, that you and I will never know God's will for our lives if we don't seriously seek it out. As one preacher put it, "God does not reveal himself to triflers."

If we sincerely *want* to know God's will, we will need to keep close to God by studying God's Word, the Bible, where God's will is revealed, and by praying, and by searching earnestly and by joining others in worship.

Receiving the blessing of knowing God's will is like having a little AM/FM transistor radio in your pocket. If you have one of those little radios, you can pick up a radio station from Hyannis.

But if you go too far away the signal peters out. The radio tower is still transmitting. It's just that you have moved too far away. Sometimes we are confused about God's will for our lives simply because we have moved too far from God (Charles Allen, *God's Psychiatry*, Spire Books, p. 108). Can we find the will and a way to move back closer, so God can reach us again?

The most perfect acceptance of God's will ever was shown by Jesus in the Garden of Gethsemane. Jesus knew what was ahead for him: that hideous, humiliating cross. He wasn't eager to suffer and die. Who would be? Why should he be? Yet Jesus prayed: "Father ... if you will, if *you* will, take this cup of suffering away from me. Not my will, not my will, however, but your will be done" (Luke 22:42 TEV, with repeats for emphasis).

Jesus knew God's will will always be done. Jesus knew God's will is always good. Jesus trusted God's will and God's goodness, even though the human part of him might not always have completely understood them.

God used that willing obedience to work something truly wonderful: after the cross, the resurrection, and our salvation, too!

"Thy will be done": can we pray it and mean it? Can we trust that God sees the big picture, that God wants what's best for us *and* for all? Will we struggle to know God's will, and to do it courageously, even if the path ahead is murky?

Simply praying, "Thy will be done," and really meaning it, might just be the most significant thing any one of us ever accomplishes in his or her life.

6

"Give Us This Day Our Daily Bread"

Today marks the mid-point of a journey. We're halfway through an extended series on the Lord's Prayer. Already we've been to the mountaintop. We've considered what it means to have God as our Father in heaven: a loving parent who knows us, who provides for us, and who longs to guide us. We've lifted up the importance of hallowing God's name. Respecting God is like a tent pole that holds up everything else. We've looked out over the expanse of God's Kingdom. We've considered what it might mean to live in it. We've thought about the joys and challenges of accepting and doing God's will.

We've been to the high peaks of the Lord's Prayer. Soon we will probe its deep valleys. "Deep calls to deep" as we consider what it means to pray for forgiveness, for avoiding temptation, and for escape from evil. Then the Lord's Prayer ends on *another* mountain top, with that soaring benediction: "For thine is the Kingdom, and the power, and the glory, forever. Amen." There *are* high peaks and deep valleys in the Lord's Prayer, aren't there?

But *today* we find ourselves with our feet planted firmly on the ground. Right in the middle of the greatest prayer ever offered, we pause — and pray for bread. Can anything be more plain or mundane than a slice of bread? Bread is so ordinary, so commonplace. So some commentators try to spiritualize this petition. They say, "When Jesus taught us to pray 'Give us this day our daily bread,' he was really telling us pray for himself: 'The bread of life' " (John 6:35b RSV).

But I don't think the bread we are supposed to pray for is spiritual. I believe Jesus wants us to pray every day for plain old bread. And that praying for bread is in itself a spiritual exercise — just as much as praying for forgiveness or hallowing God's name. Jesus had a gift for making the common uncommon. To him, nothing was ever trivial, including a piece of bread.

"Give us this day our daily bread." What are we praying for when we say this? Those words are *so* significant we must study them one by one. Let's begin with "bread." To the people of Jesus' day, "bread" was more than just yeast, water, and flour. "Bread" symbolized *everything* human beings needed for survival.

That means it's okay to pray for *all* the things that we need to live. That includes our daily bread, of course — but also clothing, employment, transportation back and forth to work, and a warm house on a cold day. To pray for "bread" is also to pray for friendship. For none of us could survive without emotional support.

"Give us this day our daily bread" tells us it's okay to pray for ourselves. That's a good reminder. For sometimes we may shy away from praying for ourselves. James B. Notkin, a pastor at University Presbyterian Church in Seattle, tells of a revelation that came to him in grade school. Notkin was running for some prestigious class office: either door monitor or eraser cleaner. The class had an election. Notkin lost — by one vote.

He went home that afternoon and told his mother. She asked him a simple question: "Well, did you vote for yourself?" Notkin says, "Now, that was a novel thought! Can you do that? Is that fair?" Voting for yourself seemed so self-centered. On reflection Notkin realized it was okay. Since then he *has* always voted for himself ("Our Bread," University Presbyterian Church audiotape, August 18, 1996).

It's always okay to pray for ourselves, for God understands what we need for survival. Jesus himself was poor. His parables are filled with references to being poor. There's the widow who barely had two nickels to rub together, and who gave them to the Temple. There's the housewife who tore apart her house just to find a lost coin. There's a parable about patching clothing. Mary must have patched Jesus' clothing.

Plus Jesus knew the stresses of providing for a family. After Joseph died, he supported his widowed mother and younger siblings by the strength of his arms, the skill of his hands, and the sweat of his brow. W. Phillip Keller writes,

> *Hacking and chopping, sawing and planing, shaping and fitting the tough, twisted olive wood and hard, heavy*

acacia timber that grew in Galilee was no child's play. It was back-breaking toil that turned trees into cattle yokes, plows, tables, and candlesticks that (Jesus) could sell for a few shekels to buy bread. (*A Layman Looks at the Lord's Prayer*, World Wide Publications, p. 102)

God understands what we need for survival. God knows the stresses of providing for a family. It's okay to pray for ourselves.

Notice, however, in the second place, that we are told to pray for daily bread, *daily* bread, *not* a stockpile of bread (or security, or things) to last us forever. By the rest of the world's standards, we Americans are fabulously rich. But it can become easy to be tied down by, or entangled in things.

Remember Gulliver in Lilliput in Jonathan Swift's *Gulliver's Travels*? Remember the scene where he was asleep on a beach, and the tiny Lilliputians tied him up? They used their strongest cords, which were only as strong as our thread. Gulliver could easily have snapped dozens. But he became immobilized because he was bound by hundreds of threads.

So also can you and I become entangled, bound up, immobilized by overconcern for our possessions. Every thing we own, from our house to our computer to our cars to the family silver, ties us down a bit, doesn't it? For it must be paid for, insured, protected, and maintained. It's like that well-known adage about owning a boat: You don't own a boat. The boat owns you.

"Give us this day our daily bread" is a prayer to God for enough — but for *only* enough. It's a prayer for simplicity. "God, give us what we need *daily*, yes! But not so much that the things we own start owning us."

In the third place, please note that we pray for *our* bread. It's plural. Just as we pray for ourselves, so also we must pray for others. Right here on comfortable Cape Cod, and around the globe, many lack adequate food, clothing, shelter, safety, emotional encouragement, and meaningful work. In fact, right now, millions are crying out to God in earnest: "Give us this day our daily bread" — because they haven't eaten today, or yesterday, or the day before.

We are called not only to pray for the hungry, but also to feed the hungry. Listen to this little poem. Jesus speaks:

*When I come in the guise
of the needy, the helpless,
the cold and the hungry,
the stranger, the lonely
will you look away?*
    What will you do?
    What will you say?

*When I come close to home
in the need of your neighbor,
at times inconvenient,
in places and faces
that mask and conceal me ...*
    What will you do?
    What will you say?

*When I come in the message
of prophet and preacher,
in truths inescapable
or words which dismay,
will you listen to me
and give me welcome?*
    What will you do?
    What will you say?

*When, face to face
at the end of the journey
we look at each other,
will you look away?*
    What will I do?
    What will I say?
(From *Bread of Tomorrow: Praying with the World's Poor*, Janet Morely, editor, SPCK, pp. 22-23)

    That's a powerful reminder that reaching out to the "least and last" among us is, in reality, reaching out to Jesus. We are meant to *pray* for each other's bread — and to *give* each other bread.

    We have considered "bread," "daily," and "our." Now we turn at last to the first word in this petition: "give." "Give us this day our daily bread." That's a reminder that *everything* we have comes to us as a gift. You and I are at every instant utterly dependent on others. We wouldn't have our daily bread at all if it weren't for the farmers and millers and bakers and warehousemen and truckers and store clerks who bring it to us.

Plus no one would have anything to share if God hadn't provided it first. Behind the farmer who grows the wheat is God who created the seed and the soil. Our Lord's prayer reminds us of our utter dependence on God.

Now we Americans may have trouble dealing with our dependence — perhaps especially native New Englanders. Many of us have been raised on rugged individualism. As the license plate of my home state, New Hampshire, puts it: "Live free or die." Legend has it, by the way, that those license plates are stamped out by prisoners in the state prisons: just another way of doing hard time in the Granite State!

We may not like to admit our dependence on others. Could that be why some men would rather drive around the block for hours than stop and ask for directions? But consider the seagull and how it soars. Have you ever gone down to Corporation Beach and watched the gulls fly?

How do gulls fly so high and so far with a bare minimum of effort? Do they flap their wings frantically? No! Well, only on takeoff. Otherwise (especially this time of year, when the wind is strong) they let the air currents carry them up.

Do we feel sorry for seagulls because they depend on wind currents? I don't. I admire them for their ability to make use of what is given them. Day by day God gives us what we need for our survival — and not just enough for us to get by but enough for us to soar.

Lord, teach us to pray, "Give us this day our daily bread." Help us to trust you to give us enough — but not overmuch. Strengthen our commitment to bring bread and peace to others. Make us wise enough to acknowledge, with thanksgiving, our dependence on you.

The Lord's Prayer brings all of God to all of life: including our need for daily bread. That's not pedestrian. It's profound. It's uplifting. It can even help us to soar.

7

"Forgive Us Our Debts As We Forgive Our Debtors"

"Forgive us our debts as we forgive our debtors." I don't know about you, but *I* find the *second part* of that petition much harder than the *first*. I find it relatively easy to ask God for forgiveness. I need God's forgiveness every day, just like I need my daily bread. But I sometimes have trouble forgiving others. What about you? Do you sometimes find it hard to forgive?

Have you ever found yourself reliving a painful incident again and again, as if you were watching a videotape in your head over and over? Have you ever fantasized, yearned for, or plotted revenge? Ever reveled in revenge? Have you ever let a wound fester, picking at it again and again so it never heals completely? Or am I the only one?

Consider this story. After the Civil War, Robert E. Lee, the former Confederate Commander, visited Kentucky. Lee stopped at a local woman's farm. She brought Robert E. Lee to her front yard and pointed out what was left of a once magnificent old tree. The woman cried bitterly because Union artillery fire had destroyed its trunk and branches.

The woman expected Robert E. Lee to join her in condemning "those damn Yankees." But after a brief silence, Lee simply said, "Cut it down, my dear madam, and forget it." Good advice: I know — we all know — there are some things we should just "cut down and forget."

But when people hurt us and the wounds are deep, *how* can we forgive them? Jesus tells us to forgive. But he doesn't say *how* to forgive. So maybe many of us, myself included, need a refresher course in forgiveness. I'd like to offer one, based on my personal reading over the last week. Let's call it "Forgiveness 101 — The Four Foundations To Forgiving."

The first foundation to forgiveness is — if we're ever going to forgive — we really have to *want* to. It can be tempting, even comfortable, to hold onto a grudge, can't it? Like a character in Robert Burns' poem, "Tam o' Shanter," we may nurse our "wrath to keep it warm." Frederick William I, King of Prussia was on his deathbed. His pastor encouraged William to forgive his enemies if he wanted to go to heaven. Frederick thought immediately of his despised brother-in-law, King George II of England. Frederick told his wife reluctantly, "In that case, write to your brother and tell him I forgive him. But," he continued, "be sure not to do it until after my death" (*The Little, Brown Book of Anecdotes*, Clifton Fadiman, editor, Little Brown, p. 223). Frederick didn't really want to forgive!

But harboring hurts and building up bitterness is toxic to us, isn't it? Booker T. Washington was right when he said, "I will not permit any man to narrow and degrade my soul by making me hate him." Another wise person, Hannah Moore, wrote, "If I had an enemy whom I wanted to punish, I would teach him to hate someone." Or, as Buddha put it, holding onto anger is like grabbing a hot coal in our hand with the intention of throwing it at someone. We're the ones who end up being burned.

There's a Russian folk tale about a mean man who went to hell. He found himself waist deep in a lake of fire. The tortured man begged the avenging angel for relief. The angel asked the mean man if he could remember doing even one merciful thing in his lifetime. The tortured man thought and thought — and finally remembered once giving an onion to a hungry beggar.

So the angel held out an onion and told the man to grab it. He did. Then the angel began to pull the man out of Hell. Several of his fellow sufferers saw what was happening and clung to the man's legs, hoping to escape with him. But he began to kick and struggle, shouting, "It's my onion! It's my onion." The onion fell apart, and the man fell back into the lake of fire. The first foundation of forgiveness is clinging to it: really *wanting* to forgive someone, if not for his or her sake, then at least for ours.

According to what I've read, forgiveness foundation two is "be realistic." Being realistic has two parts. One is acknowledging our hurt. Sometimes we are hurt but deny it. We can be like the woman who said, "I'm so glad I got religion. I've got an uncle I used to hate so much I vowed I would never go to his funeral. But, now I'd be happy to go to his funeral anytime!" Do you think that woman ever really acknowledged her anger toward her uncle?

"Forgiveness," as someone once put it, "is no duck's back." Few of us get hurt and it just rolls off us. It's okay to acknowledge to ourselves and others, "That hurt! *I'm* hurt." But we also must guard against taking some injury and blowing it way out of proportion. As Walter Wangerin, Jr., put it, we can "dump a thousand grievances into a single pot of sin" (*As For Me and My House*, Thomas Nelson, p. 97).

Say someone slights us. We can see that slight as an isolated incident. Or it can become the magnet that collects every slight we have ever received since childhood. Then, remembering all those past hurts, we can blow up at the person who has hurt us in the present. If we are to forgive, we need to be realistic: acknowledging the offense, but keeping it in perspective.

Forgiveness foundation three: surrender your right to get even. This is hard. For when we are wronged, every bone in our body cries out, "That's not fair!" Ever bump a little child accidentally? Almost instantaneously the child wells up with anger or tears or both. When we're hurt, the little child inside us cries out for justice. We want the scales balanced. And we may well *deserve* justice. It can be hard to let go of that. But it seems we have to, if we're going to forgive.

Does that mean we shouldn't confront people or hold them accountable for hurting us? No. Sometimes, if the relationship is strong enough, it's quite appropriate, even healthy, to confront the people who hurt us, telling them specifically how they hurt us and how we feel about it. But if we do so, we must do so carefully, with humility, gentleness, and love. It might help to remember the point of this little poem:

> *Has God deserted heaven*
> *And left it up to you,*
> *To judge if this or that is right*
> *And what each one should do?*

I think (God's) still in business
And knows when to wield the rod,
So when you're judging others,
Just remember, you're not — God.
(Quoted by Charles L. Allen in *God's Psychiatry*, Spire Books, p. 116)

You and I are not God. Although we're sinned against, we're also sinners. Can we remember that every day we need forgiveness ourselves?

Abraham Lincoln once received a letter from a man begging for a pardon. Lincoln was surprised there were no character references or letters of recommendation with the request. "Has this man no friends?" Lincoln asked his assistant. "No, Sir, he hasn't," the assistant responded. "Then I will be his friend," Abe said, and signed the pardon (reported by David L. Williamson in *The Library of Distinctive Sermons, volume 5*, Questars Publishers, pp. 259-60).

Before we lash out at another, can we remember that God has been our friend in those moments when *we've* been friendless? Can we remember that God has pardoned us for our sins that sent Christ to the Cross?

On the Cross, Jesus surrendered his right to get even. He could have called on twelve legions of angels to defend him (Matthew 26:53). But he didn't. Even on the cross, with nails in his hands and feet, he forgave his enemies: "Father, forgive them; for they know not what they do" (Luke 23:34 RSV).

But you and I are among those Christ has forgiven! Can't we, then, who have been loved to death (his death) by Jesus, forgive someone else for Christ's sake? Can't we surrender our right to get even? And if and when we do confront someone, can we do it in a spirit of humility, gentleness, and love?

As I understand it, the first three foundations of forgiveness are 1) really wanting to forgive; 2) being realistic about the hurt; and 3) surrendering our right to get even. The final foundation of forgiveness is "move on."

Preacher John Claypool gives us another Kentucky tree story. It seems there was a large orchard on his grandfather's farm. One day a powerful thunderstorm blew through that orchard. It blew down a pear tree that had been around for many years.

Claypool's grandfather really grieved the loss of that pear tree. He had climbed it as a boy and eaten its fruit all his life. A neighbor came over and said, "Doc, I'm really sorry to see your pear tree blown down."

"I'm sorry, too," his grandfather responded. "It was a real part of my past."

The neighbor said, "What are you going to do?"

Claypool's grandfather thought for a long moment. Then he said, "I'm going to pick the fruit and burn what's left."

John Claypool comments, "That's such a wise way of working with the past. We do need to pick its fruit. We need to learn its lessons ... But having learned what the past can teach us, we need to pick the fruit, burn what's left, and go on" ("The Future and Forgetting," *Preaching Today* Tape Number 109).

Lewis Smedes speaks of the beautiful fruits of forgiveness. By working through the foundations for forgiveness, over time "you begin to revise your feelings. The person who hurt you gradually rejoins the human race ... (You) recognize that the person who hurt you is a failed, a flawed, a fallible human being not much different from you ...."

Smedes continues, "The first time you feel you can think of the person that hurt you and just wish or pray that something good could happen to that person — maybe the good is the good that he'll never do it to anybody else — when you reach that point, you know you are on your way" to forgiveness ("Forgiveness, Doubt, Love" in *Wrestling with Angels*, Zondervan Publishing House).

Forgiveness may be difficult. But forgiveness can be fruitful.

Let us pray: God, help us to forgive our debtors as you already have forgiven our debts. Give us the grace we need to move on in the process of forgiveness. We ask in the name of Jesus Christ. Amen.

8

"Lead Us Not Into Temptation"

A mother was teaching her three-year-old daughter the Lord's Prayer. Mother recited the prayer at bedtime for several nights. The little girl followed along. Finally Mother asked her daughter if she could say the Lord's Prayer by herself.

All went well until the little girl said: "And lead us not into temptation, but deliver us some e-mail!" Like many adults, the girl had trouble with that particular line in the Lord's Prayer.

Dr. Harry Emerson Fosdick ran a radio program called *National Vespers* for almost twenty years. Each year for twenty years he received around 100,000 pieces of mail. Out of his vast experience, Fosdick wrote: "No verse in the Bible puzzles more people than the petition in the Lord's Prayer 'Lead us not into temptation.' 'Is it not a shocking idea,' many say, 'that God leads (us) into temptation and that we must beg (God) to stop...?' "

There are indeed puzzles with this part of the Lord's Prayer. This morning let's consider just two. The first is theological: "Does God tempt anyone?" The second is practical: "How can we resist temptation when it comes?"

First to the theological question: "Does God ever tempt anyone?" *Scripture* says the answer is "no." Listen to James 1:13: "No one, when tempted, should say, 'I am being tempted by God'; for God cannot be tempted by evil, and he himself tempts no one" (NRSV).

But if God tempts no one, why do we pray, "Lead us not into temptation"? Because the Greek word used here — *peirasmos* — can be translated two ways. Peirasmos can mean either "temptation" or "testing and trials." The Revised Standard Version of the Bible has "Lead us not into temptation." But the New Revised Standard Version has "Do not bring us to the time of trial."

God never tempts anyone. But God does often permit us to be tested. Why? To strengthen our character, to build our resistance, and to remind us of how dependent we are on God.

There's an old story about how a missionary candidate was tested. This young man wanted to go into overseas missions. He completed his training and was told by the Dean that he would be tested the next day. The candidate was instructed to report to the Dean's office promptly at 3:00 a.m. He did. But there was no sign of the Dean; the office was empty. He waited patiently until 9:00 a.m. when the Dean finally arrived.

There was no apology from the Dean. Instead the Dean launched into questions. First, "Can you spell 'cat'?" "C-a-t." Second, "Can you spell 'dog'?" "D-o-g." "How much is two plus two?" "Four." "Who was the first President of the United States?" "George Washington." "Congratulations," said the Dean. "You passed!"

Later that day the Dean spoke highly of that young man's character. "First I tested him on self-denial," said the Dean. "He left a warm bed to be at my office at 3 o'clock in the morning. I also tested him on punctuality. The night janitor was watching for him. He was exactly on time. Then I tried his patience. I kept him waiting six hours. But he never complained or got angry. Lastly I tested his humility. I asked him questions a child could answer. And he wasn't offended."

Life tests us often — in ways great and small. God tempts no one. But God allows us to be tested. Testing is good for us. Because faith, like a muscle, grows stronger every time it is used.

Still we pray, "Lead us not into temptation," or "Lead us not into hard testing," because we know our weakness. We know that, as Oscar Wilde put it, "(We) can resist everything except temptation." We pray that the tests God allows will not be too much.

But what about that practical question: "How can we *resist* the temptations that inevitably come to us?" It seems to me that a first step in resisting temptation is recognizing its power. Sometimes we overestimate ourselves. We're overconfident. We're like the cowpoke in the Old West: a reformed alcoholic. Unfortunately, though sober, "Slim" continued to hitch his horse to the same old hitching post in front of the saloon. Eventually the temptation to go in was too great and Slim fell off the wagon. "When it is temptation we face we are foolishly brave," as Charles Allen has said.

And sometimes it is when we are really doing well — flying high, riding the crest of a wave — that we are most in danger. "We are afraid of our weaknesses ... but ... take chances with our strengths," as someone said (Charles Allen in *God's Psychiatry*, Spire Books, p. 122).

There is a well-known story about Francis of Assisi. "Once Saint Francis and Brother Leo were out walking. Suddenly Brother Leo called out, "Brother Francis! Be careful, Brother Francis! People are saying remarkable things about you! Be careful!" Maybe it's *especially* when we're feeling strong that we most need to pray, "Lead us not into temptation." "Lead us not into the temptation of overestimating ourselves." For the higher we go spiritually, the farther we can fall.

A second step in resisting temptation is recognizing it's tricky. Sin can be quite clever in getting around our best defenses. In one of his books, Pastor Bill Barker writes about the Maginot Line. Before the Second World War the French government spent millions on a defensive line of pillboxes and forts. The French boasted that nothing could get through their defenses.

But as we know, the German blitzkrieg simply drove around the Maginot Line. The German Luftwaffe simply flew over the line. France fell to the Nazis within a few weeks (*A Savior for All Seasons*, Fleming H. Revell Company, p. 78). The French underestimated the cleverness of their enemy. *We* can underestimate the power and seductiveness of sin.

Sin is tricky. Our temptations can even change with age. Martin Luther wrote, "Young fellows are tempted by girls. Men who are thirty years old are tempted by gold. When they are forty ... (men) are tempted by honor and glory. And those who are sixty ... say to themselves, 'What a pious man I have become.' " They are tempted less by passions, but more by spiritual pride. Temptation is tricky. So we must pray, "Lead us not into temptation." "Lead us not into the temptation of ever underestimating the seductiveness of sin."

A third step in resisting temptation is not to be defeatist. We may look at the power of sin and the sneakiness of sin and decide we just can't win. So we give in. One author writes, "The biggest lie of the devil is that we *have* to sin" (Charles Allen). But we don't.

Paul writes in Philippians, "I can do all things in (Christ) who strengthens me" (4:13 RSV). God's plan for us is victory, not defeat. Plus Jesus already defeated sin — for us — on the Cross. With the help of God, and a lot of prayer, and being smart enough not to hitch our horse in front of the saloon, we can win over temptation, and not always give in to sin.

In 563 A.D. an Irish missionary named Columba landed on Iona, a bleak island off the coast of Scotland. Columba had sailed from Ireland specifically to bring the gospel to the rough inhabitants of that island and the Highlands beyond. Looking around himself, Columba realized his danger. The Scots were hostile. He was alone and frightened. Columba very much wanted to sail back to the warmth and safety of the Irish coast. Ireland *was* the intellectual and spiritual capital of Europe at the time.

What did Columba do in the face of that temptation? First he prayed. Then Columba buried his boat. So he had no other resource — or recourse — but to trust God completely. Columba put himself in God's care. God did not let him down.

Temptations are all around us. And God allows us to be tested. That testing is ultimately for our good. Often we can best those tests by not overestimating ourselves, by not underestimating the power of our enemy. And by praying fervently, burying our boats, and by putting our whole trust in God.

9

"Deliver Us From Evil"

Probably most of us are familiar with James Dickey's brilliant but disturbing novel, *Deliverance* (Dell Publishing, 1970). We've read the book or seen the film — maybe both. In *Deliverance*, four bored Atlanta suburbanites set off on a weekend canoe trip. They're amateurs. They don't know it, but the river is dangerous. So are some of the locals.

The canoe trip starts out as fun. But by the second day, things go really bad. Two grisly, gap-toothed mountain men — armed and dangerous — waylay two of the canoeists. In a brutal scene they assault one man. Then one of the other canoeists kills the mountain man with a bow and arrows they had brought along for hunting. The other mountain man is (temporarily) driven off.

Four ordinary men have a close encounter with evil. And it seems to me some of it begins to rub off. Lewis, the leader, just doesn't trust the local police. He talks the others into burying the body so that the killing — though seemingly justifiable — will never be discovered and thereby never investigated. All of them, some against their better judgment, go along. All four are now guilty of conspiracy.

As they continue down river, evil continues to lurk. For one thing, they must run dangerous, punishing rapids. Lewis is nearly killed when his canoe crashes into a rock. The river represents nature. Nature is not evil. But it is indifferent. Rivers, avalanches, hurricanes, and tornadoes do not care if human beings get in their way. Often we need deliverance from nature.

The canoeists are also stalked by the other mountain man. They shoot the rapids. He shoots at them. He kills one of the canoeists. Then one of the canoeists kills him. Again the surviving canoeists decide to hide the bodies and to tell more lies. The evil that has touched them, and infected them, spreads. By the end of their "vacation," three men are dead, one man assaulted, two injured, three bodies denied a Christian burial. And the survivors are trapped in a lifelong lie. *Deliverance* speaks to me about *our* human need for deliverance. It's realistic to pray, "Deliver us from evil." For evil is around us and inside us much of the time.

Where does evil come from? That's a question that has intrigued theologians, philosophers, and thinkers for centuries. But the Bible doesn't speculate. For, as someone once put it, if you wake up and smell smoke and find your house is on fire, you don't sit down and read a book on the origin of fire. You try your best to escape, then to put the fire out. The Bible equips us to fight the hellfire of evil. It doesn't stop to analyze where it's from.

Nor is the Bible particularly definitive on whether evil is faceless — or whether an Evil One runs it. In other words, is it "e-v-i-l"? Or should we add a "D" and make it "D-e-v-i-l"? I'm sure we all have opinions on that subject.

Scripture doesn't analyze evil. Instead it offers an assessment of our human condition. All of us, even the *best* of us, are sometimes like those canoeists: swept along by the rapids, enemies surrounding us, secrets within us. Evil is persuasive and pervasive. We need deliverance from it.

How do we fight it? To be honest, often we don't even try very hard, do we? Often we agree with Oscar Wilde: "The only way go get rid of a temptation is to yield to it." "Few speed records are broken when people run from temptation" (E. C. Mckenzie). We assume temptation is stronger than we are, and cave in.

That's the slippery slope we *all* walk. It's easy to slide down it. Sometimes it isn't the big evils that get us but the *small* temptations that slip us up. We can be like Bobbie Leach, an Englishman who went over Niagara Falls in a barrel, successfully. Not too long afterwards he slipped on a banana peel and broke his leg. Often, when faced with evil, we just give in, or slide in.

But the book of James advises us to "resist the devil, and he will flee from you" (4:7 RSV). That reminds me of something I learned about llamas, those long-necked, soft-coated creatures from Peru. Sheep ranchers in the American West were having trouble with coyotes. Sometimes the coyotes would kill fifty sheep from a flock in a year. The ranchers tried everything to get rid of coyotes: odor sprays, electric fences, loud battery radios attached to sheep's necks (probably playing rap). Nothing worked.

Today many sheep ranchers just put one lonely llama in with their sheep. Llamas, apparently, are fearless. When they see something — anything, no matter how big or dangerous it is — they just put their head down and head straight for it. Coyotes interpret that head-down advance as aggression. When faced directly, the coyotes run away.

You and I don't always need to cave in to evil. If we resist it, even for a moment, it often melts away. One pastor reminds us of Psalm 50, verse 15: "Call on me when trouble comes. I will save you," says God (quoted by Rick Warren in "How To Overcome Temptation," 7-2, "The Encouraging Word" ministries).

This same pastor encourages us, when tempted, to use a "microwave prayer." Not a long prayer: just a kind of "Help!" "Mayday!" "S.O.S.!" Warren, particularly recommends "microwave prayers" when:

> *(You) are tempted to commit a felony (because) your kids have irritated you to the limit. Or when (Y)ou're tempted to make a sarcastic reply to the boss when he blames you for his mistakes in front of other(s) ... Or when you smell the aroma of hot cinnamon buns in the mall.*

How do you spell relief? P-r-a-y-e-r. That's how Jesus resisted temptation in the desert: prayer. That's how Jesus resisted temptation in the Garden of Gethsemane: prayer. "Resist the devil, and he will flee from you." Besides, the more we resist the *stronger* our spiritual "resistance muscles" become. We don't always have to give in to sin.

Yes, we could all do better in resisting temptation. But in the end we end up — all of us — needing help. For there *are* evils stronger than our resistance: the destructive power of nature, sometimes our own body turning against us in illness. Plus there are the systemic evils of racism, chauvinistic nationalism, and economic injustice. We need a Strong Deliverer. Fortunately our Strong Deliverer is here.

Martin Luther writes of him in his great hymn:

> *Did we in our own strength confide,*
> *Our striving would be losing,*
> *Were not the right man on our side,*
> *The man of God's own choosing.*
> *Dost ask who that may be?*
> *Christ Jesus it is he;*
> *Lord Sabaoth his name.*
> *From age to age the same,*
> *And he must win the battle.*
>
> *And though this world, with devils filled,*
> *Should threaten to undo us.*
> *We will not fear, for God hath willed,*
> *His truth to triumph through us.*
> *The prince of darkness grim,*
> *We tremble not for him;*
> *His rage we can endure,*
> *For lo, his doom is sure:*
> *One little word will fell him.*

That "little word" that overcomes evil is "Easter." Evil is the great enemy of life. After all, "E-v-i–l" is "l-i-v-e" spelled backwards. On Good Friday evil tried to destroy life forever. Evil took the Prince of Light and Life and nailed him to a cross. His dead, broken body was laid in a tomb. A boulder was rolled across the mouth. It looked like evil had won.

But not for long, for Easter is God breaking the back of evil. Easter is God turning the "evil" of the cross back around into the "live" of the Risen Christ. Easter is hope and strength for us in our struggle against evil. Easter is our salvation. Easter is our deliverance. We pray, "Deliver us from evil." On Easter Sunday, God does.

Evil continues, to be sure. We can and must fight against it. Often we are stronger than we think we are. As a llama can drive away a coyote, so can we, with a little gumption, and maybe a few "microwave prayers," and the help of God, often drive away the devil.

And the devil's defeat is certain, anyway. Jesus already beat him on Easter. If we believe that and begin to live confidently in that promise, you and I can be delivered from evil.

When we encounter evil, we need not either give in to it or be afraid of it. There's a remarkable scene near the end of Charles Gounod's opera, *Faust*. Faust has sold his soul to the devil (identified in the opera as Mephistopheles). Faust draws his sword to do battle with evil. Faust isn't stronger than Mephistopheles or more clever. Nor is he quicker than the devil. Faust defeats Mephistopheles when he holds the hilt of his sword aloft so it looks like an uplifted cross. Seeing the cross, the devil cringes and retreats.

Our confidence lies not in ourselves but in the victory of Jesus Christ. "One little word shall fell him." That word is "Easter." Even the gates of Hell cannot stand against Easter. "Thanks be to God, who gives us the victory through our Lord Jesus Christ!" (1 Corinthians 15:57 RSV).

10

"For Thine Is The Kingdom And The Power And The Glory, Forever"

On a recent tour of Austria and beyond, one day our itinerary was titled "Two Churches and a Castle." One of the churches was the Wies Church, called "The Church in the Field." I've been to Bavaria before, but never before had heard of that church.

As we approached, the church *seemed* unimpressive. It is a large, hulking structure with a plain white exterior and a surprisingly squat steeple. The Wies Church looks like a totally average Bavarian parish church — just a bit bigger and set in a field, not in town.

But what a difference we discovered on the inside! The Wies Church was built in 1757 at the height of the Rococo period. Rococo is Baroque plus: very lavish, completely "over the top." Every inch of the sanctuary, from ceiling to floor, was decorated with magnificent statues, delicate plasterwork, giant frescos, paintings by masters. The predominant motif was gold and white. Solid gold or gold leaf dripped off many surfaces. Everywhere the interior was shimmering with light. If heaven is extravagant, beautifully decorated, and elaborate, then maybe we get a glimpse of heaven at Wies Church.

On the outside it was unimpressive. But the beauty of the inside was overwhelming. Some people may sometimes experience the Christian faith like that. From the outside they say, "What? Give up your Sunday morning for worship? How dull! You could be jet skiing or golfing! What? Contribute to stewardship drives and special offerings? Trading online is more fun! What? Give your time to mentor a teenager or work on an auction? And miss *Who Wants to be a Millionaire?* Or reruns of *Survivor?*

On the outside — to some — the Christian life might look dull. But it can be magnificent, overwhelming, completely fulfilling *once you're inside*. That was why, writes Distinguished Professor John Killinger, some unknown early Christians added a benediction, a doxology, to the Lord's Prayer (*The God Named Hallowed*, Abingdon Press, pp. 73-74).

"For thine is the Kingdom and the power and the glory forever" does not appear in the earliest manuscripts. Bible experts agree it was added by the later church. No matter. It was an exuberant shout of joy, an exclamation point added by believers who were looking at Christianity from the inside. They couldn't suppress their excitement and wonder — just as we had to express *our* astonishment at the inside of Wies Church.

Have you ever been in the presence of greatness and missed it? A newspaper editor from Harrisburg, Pennsylvania, 35 miles from Gettysburg, heard Abraham Lincoln deliver the Gettysburg Address. The next day the editor wrote in his paper, "We pass over the silly remarks of the President; for the credit of the nation, we are willing that the veil of oblivion shall be dropped over them and that they should no more be repeated or thought of." This man heard the Gettysburg Address delivered by Abraham Lincoln himself — and missed its significance!

Many of us have heard that story about Emperor Ferdinand of Austria, on hearing Mozart's *The Marriage of Figaro* for the first time. Ferdinand said to Mozart, "Far too noisy, my dear Mozart. Far too many notes." True greatness missed again!

Here we are worshiping in Dennis Union Church: this old New England Congregationalist meeting house with its plain walls and clear windows. This is no Rococo wedding cake wonder. But do we recognize the wonder of where we are and what we're doing?

Here's a hint. What's the road called that runs just in front of us by the Village Green? Sometimes Route 6A, sometimes Main Street, Dennis. But what was that road called when it developed from a cow path in the 1600s? *King's* Highway: or *Old* King's Highway now, because it's so old.

For this particular church in this particular place, *I* think there's a connection. Right now, this very instant, just off King's Highway, you and I are in the Kingdom, the Realm of God.

"But," some of you may be thinking, "I thought the Kingdom of God was *coming*." For we do pray, "Thy Kingdom come, thy will be done, on earth as it is in heaven." Yes, the Kingdom, the Rule of God, *is* still in the future. God's justice and righteousness have yet to be established on this planet. So in one sense we're still waiting for the Kingdom to come.

But in another sense the Kingdom of God has already come among us. Christ was born in Bethlehem. God took on human flesh. Jesus grew up to teach us — and show us — the way to live. Then he died on a cross to take away our sins. On the third day God raised him up from the dead with mighty power, so that *you and I* might live in him — forever.

In his first sermon, Jesus proclaimed, "The Kingdom of God is at hand" (Mark 1:15 RSV). It's near. It's here. We're living in God's Kingdom now. "For thine is the Kingdom and the power and the glory forever," proclaimed the Early Christians. "Forever": always and at the end times, yes, but also *now*.

What's so special about the Realm of God, God's Kingdom? For one thing, this Kingdom is forever. In the early 1800s Napoleon Bonaparte controlled most of the European continent. He crowned himself Emperor, cultivated his cult, and built the Arc de Triomphe to celebrate his victories. And why not? For a time Napoleon or his puppets ruled from Portugal to the gates of the Kremlin. Legend has it that on hearing an old Latin proverb, "Man proposes, God disposes," a boastful Napoleon corrected it: "*I* propose and (*I*) dispose, too." Napoleon put himself in the place of God! But today old Napoleon has been reduced to a finger cake!

Adolf Hitler also conquered most of Europe. He boasted he would institute a Thousand-Year German Reich. Hitler's Third Reich lasted twelve years. Twenty-five years ago the Shah ruled Iran, then a wealthy country with a mighty army. He called himself "The King of Kings, the Light of Lights" — but died an outcast, in exile, without a country, with a price on his head. Fifteen years ago Manuel Noriega had himself named "Maximum Leader." Fourteen years ago in Rumania Ceausescu, the self-styled "Genius of the Carpathians" owned 21 palaces, forty villas, and twenty hunting lodges. "O Where Are Kings and Empires Now?" the old hymn asks. Napoleon, Hitler, the Shah, Noriega, Ceausescu are all gone. No earthly power, no matter how mighty, lasts. And that includes the military, economic, and cultural supremacy of America today. You know, on our recent trip, the first restaurant we saw in the Czech Republic was a McDonalds! Budapest was overrun with American corporations and corporate signs. In much of the world the American dollar and American culture reign supreme.

But as the Methodist missionary E. Stanley Jones wrote decades ago while visiting Moscow: "I saw as in a flash that all man-made kingdoms are shakable. The kingdom of communism is shakable: they have to hold it together by purges ... they cannot relax ... or it will fall apart." E. Stanley Jones was right. But he continued, "The kingdom of capitalism is shakable (too) ... The kingdom of self is shakable ... The kingdom of health is shakable ... Everything is shakable, except one (thing) — the Kingdom of God" (from *Song of Assents*, Abingdon Press, pp. 149-150, quoted by John Killinger in *The God Named Hallowed*, Abingdon Press, p. 78).

Everything else we put our trust in will fade. Even diamonds aren't forever. Napoleon bought his Empress Josephine a diamond tiara. Within years, someone else owned it. But God's is the Kingdom and the power and the glory — forever. We are in the presence of true greatness, God's Kingdom. Do we catch the wonder?

It does make a difference if we choose to live under the rule of God, if we choose to live in God's Kingdom. For you see, living or not living in God's Kingdom is ultimately up to us. God has the Kingdom and the power and the glory to force you and me to be subjects.

God is great. God created our planet. And our planet is complicated. It moves in at least six directions at once, as I read somewhere years ago. 1) The earth spins on its axis like a top, at a thousand miles an hour. 2) The earth weaves slowly back and forth on its axis, at an angle of 23 degrees twice a year. That gives us our seasons. 3) The earth rotates yearly around the sun at a rate of 18.5 miles per second. 4) This solar system, with the earth in it, is moving what we consider northward at a rate of twelve miles per second. 5) The nearby stars, with our solar system, are revolving around the center of the Milky Way at 180 miles per second. 6) Our galaxy, the Milky Way, with its millions of stars, is on its own journey through space, moving outward.

This one tiny planet moves simultaneously in at least six directions! I'd call that an engineering feat! Bigger than the Big Dig, that fourteen billion dollar project in Boston! And on time! And at no cost to us! God planned it all and God keeps it running.

This Almighty God has the power to do anything. The great God who keeps the planets spinning could easily storm and conquer our little closed up "castles of self." God could make us take God as King. But the greatest wonder is this: that this mighty God stands outside the fast-closed doors of our hearts and patiently knocks and waits to be invited in (see Revelation 3:20). The greatest wonder is this: that the One whose Kingdom and power and glory are forever chose to come to us in the humility and worldly weakness in Jesus. On the outside he looked like a simple carpenter and preacher. But on the inside he was the mighty Power of God. God's power to save us from our sins. God's power to crush all enemies, even death.

Sometimes what's on the outside can be deceiving. Sometimes it's only when we get on the inside that we discover the real beauty and joy. Right here, right now, on the edge of King's Highway, you and I are in the presence of greatness. Do we know it? Do we understand we have a chance to live in the one Kingdom that will never end? Do we know the joy of a personal relationship daily with Jesus Christ? Many of us have been in some pretty awe-inspiring churches and cathedrals. But not even the wonder of Notre Dame can match the wonder of what is offered this morning in this little church.

Can we open the doors of our hearts to Jesus Christ and let him in, so that his beauty and his goodness might begin to cleanse us and heal us and fill us? "For thine is the Kingdom and the power and the glory forever — everywhere, even in my heart." The great "Amen" to that is to open our hearts — and open our lives — to the Kingdom of God.

11

"Amen"

(Before preaching I reminded our congregation that — in some traditions — the preacher receives encouragement from an occasional, enthusiastic "Amen!" In some liturgical traditions, like the Roman Catholic or Anglican, prayers are followed by a congregational "Amen." This Sunday I invited them to join the "Amen Corner." Every time they heard me say, "Let the people say, 'Amen,' " they were asked to respond with a loud "Amen!" The "Amen" response was practiced several times.)

"There is too much speaking in the world," wrote author Bruce Barton. "There is too much speaking in the world, and almost all of it is too long." Let the people say, "Amen." ("Amen!") Barton continues, "The Lord's Prayer, the Twenty-third Psalm, Lincoln's Gettysburg Address, are three great literary treasures that will last forever; not one of them is as long as three hundred words." Bruce Barton concludes, "With such striking illustrations of the power of brevity, it is amazing that speakers never learn to be brief." Let the people say, "Amen." ("Amen!")

This is my *eleventh* sermon on the Lord's Prayer! If I preached all eleven sermons in a row, one after the other (if anyone would listen), it would take more than two-and-a-half hours: not brief. But the topic *is* important. The Lord's prayer is the *only* prayer Jesus taught us. So here's one more sermon on the Lord's Prayer. But this series is nearly ended! Let the people say, "Amen." ("Amen!")

"Amen." That's an interesting word, isn't it? It's one four-letter word that's always good to use, like "love" or "gift." "Amen" is used everywhere on earth — and never translated. It's probably the only word ever used that means the same thing everyplace.

This word appears more than fifty times in the Bible. In fact, "Amen" is the last word in God's Word. Look it up: Revelation, chapter 22, verse 21 (NRSV). We know this word. But do we remember its meaning? "Amen" is ancient Hebrew for "so be it" or "let it be so."

"Amen" actually has a long development in scripture. It originally meant assent to a curse. In Deuteronomy (27:15), Moses is depicted as giving instructions to the people of Israel about how they should behave in the Promised Land. Once they get there, says Moses, the Levites, the Priests, are to curse anyone who makes an idol. As the idol-maker is cursed, the people add to the curse by shouting, "Amen."

"Amen" later turns from something negative (a "curse word,") into something positive: a word of agreement. In First Kings (1:36) David decides to make his son Solomon king. On hearing this, one of David's court advisors shouts out an enthusiastic "Amen!"

By the book of Psalms "Amen" evolved into a word of worship. Psalm 72:18-19: "Blessed be the Lord, the God of Israel ... Blessed be his glorious name forever ... Amen and Amen!" (RSV). What started out as an assent to a curse became a way of praising God.

In the New Testament (the Christian Scriptures) "Amen" is elevated again. In Second Corinthians, Paul says we say our "Amens" *through* Jesus (1:20b). In Revelation (3:14), Jesus himself is depicted as God's "faithful" and "true" "Amen." Jesus, the Word of Life, is the final Word of God.

From part of a curse, to a positive word, to a word of worship, to a name for Jesus, "Amen" becomes richer and richer over time. It's a mighty, ancient word of power and worship that has thousands of years of history behind it. Let all the people say, "Amen." ("Amen!")

Of course, "Amen" wasn't part of the original Lord's Prayer, was it? Like the Benediction, "For thine is the Kingdom and the power, and the glory, forever," it was added later. Still "Amen" is a fitting way to say we agree with what we pray.

Let's do a brief review of the Lord's Prayer. It begins, "Our Father, which art in heaven." Do you remember the word Jesus used for "Father" was "Abba" — and that "Abba" means "Daddy"? Jesus wants us to know that the great God of the universe is our loving Parent. Do you believe that? Can you affirm it? Would you *like* to affirm it? If you believe God is a Father/Parent who loves you and cares for you, let the people say, "Amen." ("Amen!")

The Lord's Prayer continues by reminding us that God's name should be "hallowed." To "hallow" means to "respect greatly," or to "make holy or set apart." That's the origin of the word "Halloween." "Halloween," the night before "All Saints' Day," November 1, started out as a "hallowed e'en," a "holy evening" for Christians. The church celebrated not ghosts and goblins but God's glorious saints.

Obviously we haven't "hallowed" Halloween, have we? But don't you agree we should hallow God's name? Will we try to honor the name of God by not using it as a curse? Will we honor God's name by living the way God would have us live? God's name deserves to be hallowed. If you agree with *that*, let the people say, "Amen." ("Amen!")

God invites us into God's rule, God's "Kingdom." Sometimes our lives are like a series of concentric circles. We put ourselves in the center. The needs of our family and friends come next. Next come the needs of our community and our country. The rule of God — if it's anywhere — is somewhere out on the edge.

But to pray, "Thy Kingdom come" — and really mean it — is to reverse that order. It's to put God in the center, the needs of others second, and our needs last. "Thy Kingdom come." Can we pray that and mean it? Can we strive to put God first? Let the people say, "Amen." ("Amen!")

"Thy will be done." That means acknowledging that God (Father) knows best. Sometimes God can be like that (seemingly) strict teacher we had in school, the one who insisted we try harder, who wouldn't allow let us get lazy or do less than our best. God bless you, Mrs. Gladys Sundstrom! I remember you still!

Sometimes God is like that. Sometimes God's lesson plan seems too difficult for us. Sometimes (maybe especially when "The Golden Years" aren't so "golden") we long to quit. But God is good. And God's will for us is always good. Even in the tough lessons of life, can we pray "Thy will be done"? Can we trust that

God is a wise and loving Teacher? If so, let the people say, "Amen." ("Amen!")

The first part of the Lord's Prayer lifts up God as our loving Father, worthy of reverence, whose rule is good and whose will should be followed. In the last part of the Lord's Prayer we pray for others and ourselves. We pray for our daily bread, because we need God to feed us daily. Let the people say "Amen." ("Amen!") We pray that God will forgive our sins — and that we can and will forgive. Let the people say, "Amen." ("Amen!")

We pray, "Lead us not into temptation." We know we can resist anything *except* temptation (Oscar Wilde). Let the people say, "Amen." ("Amen!") We pray, "Deliver us from evil." "Evil" is "live" spelled backwards. Evil is everything that is the enemy of life. Evil is powerful. Evil is around us. Sometimes evil is in us. We need deliverance. Let the people say, "Amen." ("Amen!")

Then we end the Lord's Prayer as we began it, by praising God: "For thine is the Kingdom and the power and the glory forever (and ever). Amen." I grew up in New Hampshire. As a child, I heard a lot about Daniel Webster, the noted New Hampshire orator and statesman. Here's one story I both heard and read. On the night of October 24, 1852, in Marshfield, Massachusetts, Daniel Webster lay dying. His personal physician was at his bed. Dr. Jeffries knew Daniel Webster was a man of deep faith. So to comfort his nearly unconscious patient, the doctor recited verses from a favorite hymn. With his last breaths, in a loud, clear voice, the great orator shouted out, "Amen! Amen! Amen!" Then he died.

After researching this story, I've discovered it's apocryphal. Still, it's a great story, isn't it? If it were true, wouldn't that be Daniel Webster's greatest speech, "Amen"? "Amen!" "Let it be so." "So be it." Can we accept God's gifts and God's goodness and God's grace — and God's will for us — not only at death but also in life? For the Lord's Prayer, just 65 words long, teaches us everything we need to know for a happy, fulfilled life. We prayed, "Lord, teach us to pray." And, Lord, you did it. You responded, "Pray like this." Thank you for the gift of the Lord's Prayer. Now we pray, "Lord, teach us to live it."

Let the people say, "Amen."

www.ingramcontent.com/pod-product-compliance
Lightning Source LLC
Chambersburg PA
CBHW071414040426
42444CB00009B/2242